I0815341

BROKEN RECORDS
SPORTS RECORDS
TO MAKE YOU CHEER!
KENNY ABDO
Fly!
An Imprint of Abdo Zoom
abdobooks.com

abdobooks.com

Published by Abdo Zoom, a division of ABDO, P.O. Box 398166, Minneapolis, Minnesota 55439.

Printed in the United States of America, North Mankato, Minnesota.
052023
092023

Photo Credits: Alamy, AP Images, Getty Images, Shutterstock
Production Contributors: Kenny Abdo, Jennie Forsberg, Grace Hansen
Design Contributors: Candice Keimig, Neil Klinepier, Laura Graphenteen

Library of Congress Control Number: 2022946922

Publisher's Cataloging-in-Publication Data

Names: Abdo, Kenny, author.
Title: Sports records to make you cheer! / by Kenny Abdo
Description: Minneapolis, Minnesota : Abdo Zoom, 2024 | Series: Broken records | Includes online resources and index.
Identifiers: ISBN 9781098281403 (lib. bdg.) | ISBN 9781098282103 (ebook) | ISBN 9781098282455 (Read-to-me ebook)
Subjects: LCSH: Records--Juvenile literature. | History--Juvenile literature. | Sports records--Juvenile literature.
Classification: DDC 032.02--dc23

TABLE OF CONTENTS

SPORTS RECORDS

Professional athletes have always wowed audiences with their skills. But when they break world records, it's a whole new ball game!

OMEGA
OMEGA
11

From incredible running speeds to unbreakable **hitting streaks**, these sports records will get crowds cheering!

BROKEN RECORDS

New York Yankees center fielder Joe DiMaggio had a great season in 1941. He recorded at least one hit in 56 straight games.

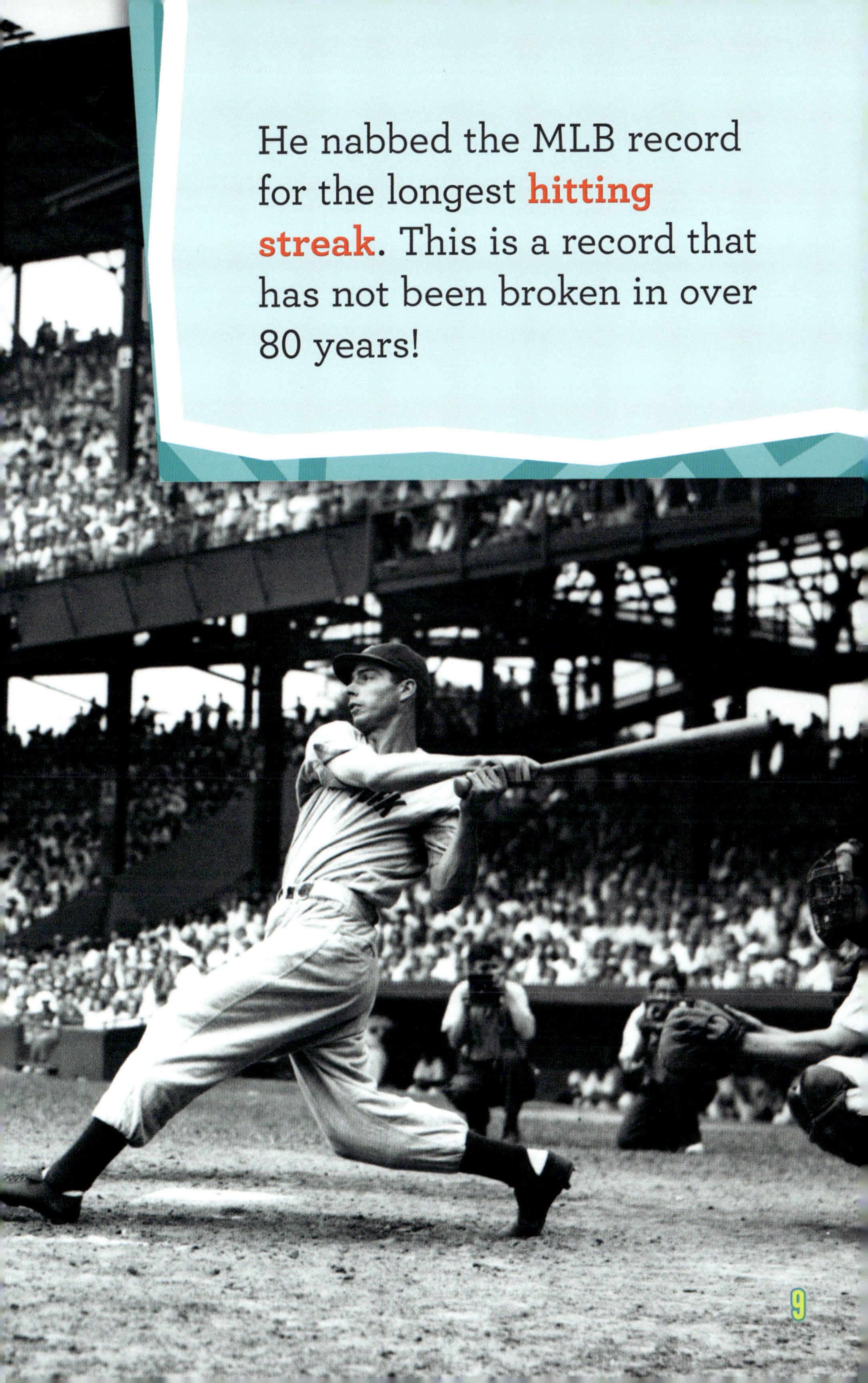

He nabbed the MLB record for the longest **hitting streak**. This is a record that has not been broken in over 80 years!

ROMANIA

Nadia Comăneci made history at the 1976 Montreal **Olympics**. The 14-year-old Romanian gymnast was the first to be awarded a perfect 10 score. Comăneci also earned the **Guinness World Record** for being the first!

Runner Usain Bolt shocked the world at the 2009 Berlin World Athletics **Championship**. He broke the record for fastest time running the 100-meter dash. Reaching 28 mph (44.7 km/h) in just 9.58 seconds, he blew past the competition!

HAVE A GOOD TIME!
SAMSUNG

Red Bull

Max Verstappen became the youngest driver to win a Formula One World **Championship**. He reached first place at the 2016 Spanish Grand Prix. Verstappen was only 18 years old!

Serena Williams won her first **Grand Slam** singles **title** in 1999. She nabbed her 23rd at the 2017 Australian Open. Williams owns the record for longest span of Grand Slam singles titles, along with many other **Guinness World Records**!

In 2023, Tottenham Hotspur **striker** Harry Kane entered the history books. He scored his 267th goal for the team. Kane became the player to score the most career goals for a single club in the **English Premier League**!

FOR THE RECORD

Athletes continue to inspire their fans by being the best at what they do. And sometimes, they knock world records out of the park!

GLOSSARY

championship – an event held to find a first-place winner.

English Premier League – the professional soccer organization that includes the top teams in England and Wales.

Grand Slam – winning all four major championships in the same calendar year.

Guinness World Record – an award given to those who have broken a record never achieved before.

hitting streak – in baseball, the consecutive number of official games in which a player gets at least one base hit.

Olympic Games – the biggest international athletic event held as separate winter and summer competitions every four years in a different city.

striker – in soccer, the player who plays closest to the opponent's goal.

title – a first-place position in a contest.

ONLINE RESOURCES

To learn more about sports records, please visit **abdobooklinks.com** or scan this QR code. These links are routinely monitored and updated to provide the most current information available.

INDEX